Living in
Australia

Written and photographed by
David Hampton

FRANKLIN WATTS
LONDON • SYDNEY

First published in 2002 by
Franklin Watts,
96 Leonard Street,
London EC2A 4XD

Franklin Watts Australia,
56 O'Riordan Street,
Alexandria, NSW 2015

Copyright © Franklin Watts 2002

Series editor: Ruth Thomson
Series designer: Edward Kinsey
Additional photograph: Bridget Sherlock 8(c)

A CIP catalogue record for this book is
available from the British Library
Dewey Classification 919.4

ISBN 0 7496 4643 8

Printed in Malaysia

Contents

This is Australia

Australia is the only country in the world that is also a continent. It is a huge island surrounded by sea. Tasmania, a small island off the south coast, is also part of Australia.

The country is divided into eight regions – six states and two territories. Tasmania is one of the states.

△**Rainforest**
Rainforest covers vast areas of Northern Queensland. Some is being cut down to make way for farming and mining.

△**Desert**
Much of the west and centre of Australia is desert or semi-desert, with vast salt pans. Less than 500mm of rain falls there per year.

▷**Cities**
Seven of the biggest cities are on the coast.

Fact Box

Capital: Canberra
Population: 18.5 million
Official language: English
Main religion: Christianity
Highest mountain: Mount Kosciusko (2,228m)
Longest river: Darling (2,739km)
State capitals: Sydney, Perth, Melbourne, Brisbane, Adelaide, Hobart
Territory capitals: Canberra, Darwin
Currency: Australian dollar

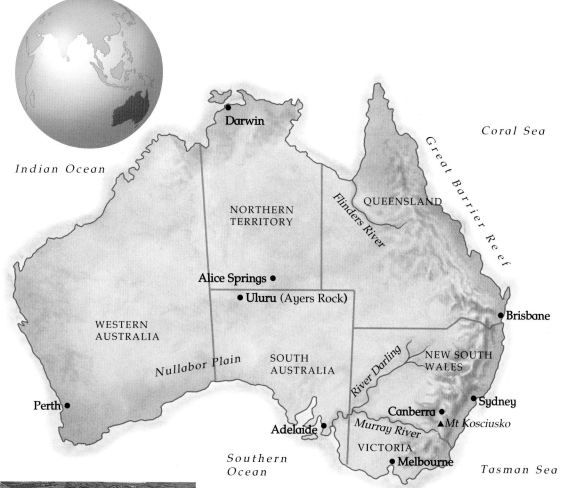

△**People**
The Aborigines are the first known inhabitants of Australia. Since the first Europeans arrived in 1788, people from more than 200 countries have made Australia their home.

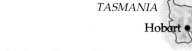

◁**Coral reefs**
There are coral reefs off the western and eastern coastline. The largest is the Great Barrier Reef.

◁**Mountains**
The Blue Mountains, west of Sydney, are often covered with cloud. The water vapour in the air makes them appear blue.

5

Canberra – the capital

Canberra is the capital of Australia. This small city was built from scratch in the early 1900s as the new place of government. Before this, Melbourne had been the capital. Canberra was designed by an American architect, who won a competition to create this new city.

△**The Australian crest**
A kangaroo and an emu, the national animal and bird, are part of the crest of Australia.

▷**Parliament House**
The government meets in Parliament House, which was built in 1988. The old Parliament building is now the National Portrait Gallery.

△**Aboriginal embassy**
This building, near the old Parliament, is a reminder that the Aborigines are unhappy about the way they are treated by the mainly white government.

▷Lake Burley Griffin
This man-made lake is named after the architect who planned the city. It was created by damming a nearby river.

▽War memorial
This building is a tribute to the 102,600 people who have died in wars whilst serving their country.

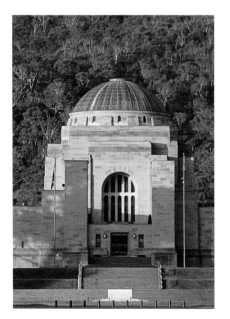

▷A view of the city
The view of the capital from Mount Ainslie is popular with the thousands of tourists who visit Canberra every year.

Famous sights

Australia is famous for its unique wildlife, especially marsupials, such as the kangaroo, wallaby and koala.

The country is also well-known for its fantastic beaches, unusual landscape and friendly people, as well as for important Aboriginal landmarks.

△**Koala**
The koala is a nocturnal mammal that lives in forests. It eats only the leaves of one species of eucalpytus tree.

Baby kangaroo (joey)

8

△**Aboriginal art**
There are Aboriginal cave paintings in the Kakadu National Park in the Northern Territory. Some are thought to be more than 20,000 years old.

◁**Uluru**
Uluru (Ayers Rock) rises from the flat desert about 250km from Alice Springs. It is a sacred site for Aborigines. It appears to change colour throughout the day.

△Bondi beach

Bondi is Sydney's most famous beach. People come here from all over the world to surf on the waves that roll in from the Tasman Sea.

◁The Great Barrier Reef

The Great Barrier Reef is a huge tourist attraction. People dive and snorkel around the reef, watching the shoals of tropical fish.

△Sydney Opera House

The Sydney Opera House is a series of concert halls and theatres. It stands overlooking Sydney Harbour. Its shape was inspired by sea shells.

Living in cities

Almost nine out of ten Australians live in towns or cities, and within 80km of the sea. Most families own houses in the suburbs. The houses are usually detached, built of brick and have large gardens. In recent years, high-rise apartments have been built near city centres. These are for people who want to live close to where they work.

△**The police**
Each state has its own police force. This policeman patrols the park in a buggy that has a sunshade.

△**Suburbs**
Most cities are very spread out. Gardens have tall trees to provide shade for homes.

◁**Town houses**
New homes often have huge balconies or verandahs where people can sit out. To save space, houses may have a two-car garage underneath.

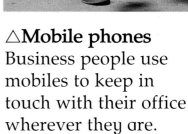

△Mobile phones
Business people use mobiles to keep in touch with their office wherever they are.

△City centres
Banks, offices, restaurants, department stores and other shops are concentrated in city centres. The streets are crowded at lunchtimes and at rush hours.

Brochures for city sights

11

Living in the outback

Australians call the countryside the *bush* or the *outback*. Very few people live here. In hot, dry places, few crops can grow and fresh water is scarce.

Properties and towns may be hundreds of kilometres apart.

△Mailbox
Some cattle and sheep farms (*stations*) in the remotest parts of the outback have mailboxes as far as 150km away from the house.

▷Homesteads
Most farmhouses (*homesteads*) are built of timber with corrugated iron roofs. Outbuildings house workers who come to help farmers at busy times of year, such as sheep shearing.

△Cattle ranching
This man and his family run a cattle station that covers thousands of square kilometres. It takes them more than six hours to drive to the nearest town.

12

◁**Collecting water**
This woman from the far north has to collect water from a spring a long walk from her home.

▽**Artesian water**
Outback homes mainly rely on water pumped up from underground by windmills. The water is warm and salty. It must be filtered before it can be drunk.

△**An outback town**
Many people visit town only a few times a year. They stock up with packaged foods. Most of them travel in a four-wheel drive vehicle, called a utility (*ute*).

▽**Flying Doctor Service**
Distances between places in the outback are so great that planes are used to take people to hospital in emergencies.

13

Working in the outback

Sheepskin boot

Most people in the outback work in either farming or mining.

Farmers mainly keep sheep or cattle. Cereal crops, especially wheat, and fruit, such as apples and oranges, are grown for export.

△Sheep
Australia is home to about 150 million sheep. It is the world's biggest exporter of wool and meat.

▷Cattle
These cattle in the Northern Territory are being taken to market. This is a long, hard, hot and dusty job for the horseback riders.

△Sugar
Sugar cane, grown in Queensland, is one of Australia's most important crops. Many towns have a refinery where the cane is processed into sugar.

14

▽▷Grapes

Grapes, grown in the south and east, are mostly used for wine. These grapes are being dried in the sun and will be packaged as sultanas.

△Loading up

This huge truck is being loaded with bauxite. This will be smelted and used to make aluminium.

Iron ore

Bauxite

Lead ore

Mining

Iron and lead ore, bauxite, silver, gold and coal are dug from Australia's many mines, along with precious diamonds and opals. These are exported all over the world.

A sporting nation

As the weather is generally warm, Australians take part in all sorts of outdoor sports. They excel particularly at water sports, such as swimming, sailing and wind-surfing. In 2000, Sydney hosted the Olympic Games.

△ Aussie Rules
This popular game combines the rules of soccer and rugby. There are 18 players on each side.

▷ Tennis
Children learn tennis from a young age. These boys are coached three nights a week and play matches at weekends.

△ Cricket
Cricket is a popular spectator sport. Every city, town and village has its own team. The Australian team often wins the International Test Match series.

▷Surf life-saving

Most beaches have
a life-saving club.
Members take it in turn
to watch out for people
in trouble. The clubs
hold races in the surf
kayaks used for rescue.

▽Beach flags

Brightly coloured
flags show bathers
where it is safest
to swim or surf.

△Sailing

Yacht racing has
become increasingly
popular since an
Australian yacht
won the America's
Cup in 1983.

◁Surfing

Australian waves are
some of the biggest
in the world. They
are ideal for surfing.

Shopping

Towns still have lots of high street shops. In cities, these are being replaced by out-of-town shopping centres or inner-city malls. The wide range of shops and products reflects the differing tastes and lifestyles of the multi-cultural population.

△**Shopping streets**
Shops often have flat roofs that extend over the pavement. These protect shoppers from sun and rain.

△**Markets**
At weekends, street markets are a feature of many towns and cities. Often hot food and snacks are available.

▷**Fruit shops**
Fruit is almost entirely homegrown. Tropical fruits, such as bananas, pineapples and mangoes, grow in the north and east.

Pineapple

△Food shops
In cities, it is quite common to see Chinese, Greek, Indian and Jewish food shops side by side in the same street.

▽Homegrown food
All these products come from crops grown on the rich farmlands of the east coast.

Tomato sauce

Tinned fruit

Orange juice

Yeast extract

Dollars

Cents

△Australian currency
Australians use dollars and cents.

△▷Convenience stores
Convenience stores sell sweets, lottery tickets, phone cards and newspapers, as well as food. Foreign language newspapers are sold in all big cities.

Phone card

Lottery tickets

Sweets

On the move

Transport systems are very modern and well-organised. Major roads link the major cities of every state. Most families own two cars.

Melbourne, Adelaide and Brisbane have trams. Sydney has a monorail.

△Trains
Trains are still used to carry freight, but, because of the huge distances, most people fly from city to city.

△City roads
New, multi-lane highways link the suburbs to city centres. These help the flow of inner-city traffic.

◁Monorail
The monorail in the centre of Sydney links the shopping and business districts.

Distance
sign

◁Road or airstrip?
In times of emergency, some roads in the outback double as airstrips for the Royal Flying Doctor Service.

▽A road train
Huge trucks with three linked trailers move goods across the country. A road train can transport hundreds of sheep or cattle at a time.

Roads in the outback
The distances between places in the outback can be enormous. There is very little traffic on the roads, so most of them are single-lane.

Family life

Most families enjoy a comfortable way of life. Their homes are spacious and well-equipped with fridges, freezers and other modern appliances.

People work hard in the week, but rarely at weekends. Families enjoy spending their time off together.

▽**Watching television**
Almost every family has a television and watching sport is very popular. The Australian soaps, *Home and Away* and *Neighbours,* are watched worldwide.

Weekly TV magazine

△**Swimming pools**
Many homes have enough space in the garden for a large swimming pool.

▷Bedrooms

Modern homes have at least four bedrooms and two bathrooms. Children usually have their own room.

◁Clothes drying

Washing never takes long to dry in the warm climate, especially in the north and west, where temperatures can reach 40° C.

▷Texting

People text their friends on their mobiles. Phone charges are quite low compared with those in most other developed countries.

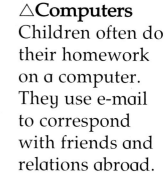

△Computers

Children often do their homework on a computer. They use e-mail to correspond with friends and relations abroad.

Time to eat

A traditional Australian meal includes meat, vegetables and a dessert. However, people now eat dishes from all over the world, especially those from different parts of Asia. The city of Sydney claims that visitors could eat in a different ethnic restaurant every day of the year, without ever eating food from the same place twice!

△Breakfast
A great favourite at breakfast is a bowl of cereal with milk, sugar and fresh fruit.

▷Barbecues
People take advantage of the warm climate and eat outside as often as possible. They cook steak, lamb or fish over hot charcoal on a barbecue (*barbie*).

△Barbecue food
Barbecues aren't complete without a selection of fresh salads, crisps and biscuits called brownies.

Meat pie

△Takeaway food

Meat pies are the traditional snack. These are being replaced by foods from around the world. (Roast *chooks* are roast chicken.)

▽Restaurants

Eating out is very informal. Cafés and restaurants often have outside seating. In big cities, there are ethnic restaurants of all kinds.

△Snack bars

City commuters often start their day with coffee and cakes at a snack bar.

▷Fish

There is a plentiful supply of fresh fish, such as tuna and mullet. Shellfish are farmed off the coast. Tiger prawns are a favourite – they only turn pink when they are cooked.

Cooked tiger prawns

Raw tiger prawns

School time

Education in Australia is free. It is compulsory for most children between the ages of 5 and 15. However, some Aboriginal parents choose not to send their children to state schools. Instead, they educate them in the traditions of their own culture at home.

▽In class
Lessons begin at 8.30 or 9 am and continue until 3 or 3.30 pm. There are always after-school activities and sports.

△Going to school
Children who live near school may walk or cycle there. Many schools provide locked, covered bike racks for cyclists.

◁School buses
Children who live a long way from school may have to get up early to catch a school bus. The ride may take up to an hour.

SCHOOL BUS ROUTE

NEXT 17 km

◁**Learning outside**
When they have lessons outside, children have to wear hats to protect them from the hot sun.

Maths book

Learning at a distance

In the remote outback, some children are taught over the radio by the School of the Air. Each pupil has a radio set at home and talks for up to five hours a day to the teacher and other pupils. Children, parents and teachers meet several times a year to discuss the pupils' progress.

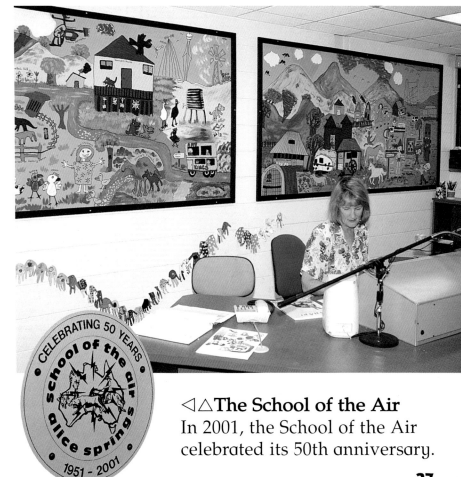

◁△**The School of the Air**
In 2001, the School of the Air celebrated its 50th anniversary.

Having fun

Australians are a particularly fun-loving nation. They enjoy the outdoor life and almost everything they do in their spare time reflects this. There are national parks in every state. These are a popular place to spend time trekking or exploring during the long school holidays in the summer (around Christmas-time).

△Camping
There are camping and caravan sites all over Australia. These are well-used, especially at weekends.

△Beach volleyball
Teams, especially life-saving teams, play volleyball on the beach. Running in soft sand helps them keep fit.

▷Fishing
Fishing for sport is popular both in the sea and on rivers. The freshly caught fish are cooked on barbecues.

Suncream

Sunglasses

△Sun protection
The sun can be very hot, so people are careful to put on suncream and wear sunglasses.

△Cycling
Families use mountain bikes to explore the rugged landscape.

◁Basketball
Even children in remote outback communities may have a basketball court.

△Theme parks
People enjoy dare-devil rides in city theme parks.

Going further

Aboriginal painting

Lots of Aboriginal paintings are made by using the end of a stick instead of a brush.

Look closely at the boomerang and use the same painting technique to make your own pictures and designs.

Sweet wrappers

The Australian chocolate bars below each feature a different Australian animal.

Design some sweet wrappers, using a different Australian theme – for example sport or famous sights.

A fire poster

Fire is one of the greatest dangers to life and property in Australia.

Design a poster to encourage people not to light fires when the weather is very hot and dry.

Websites

www.about-australia.com
www.frogandtoad.com.au
www.auslig.gov.au

Glossary

Artesian water Water that has been taken from underground.

Commuter Someone who travels some distance from home to work each day.

Continent One of the large landmasses of the world.

Coral reef A bank of coral just below sea-level.

Crest An official badge.

Currency The money used in a country.

Exporter Someone who sells a product from one country to another.

Marsupial A mammal that carries its young in a pouch.

Monorail A railway with only one rail.

Nocturnal Active at night.

Ore A solid, rock-like material which contains a valuable metal.

Population The number of people who live in one place.

Rainforest A lush, dense forest found in hot regions with high rainfall.

Refinery A place where raw materials are turned into a product.

Smelt To melt ore to extract metal from it.

State A region of a country that has its own government for local affairs.

Suburbs Housing on the outer areas of a city.

Territory A region of a country that has its own government for local affairs, like a state.

Verandah A covered space along the side of a building.

Index